Life is Better
in the *Pause*

TRACEY CRUZ

Mission: To Proclaim Transformation and Truth
Publisher: Transformed Publishing, Cocoa, FL
Website: www.transformedpublishing.com
Email: transformedpublishing@gmail.com

Illustrations retrieved from Storyblocks.com by publisher (subscription plan March 2023).

Scripture marked NIV, was taken from the New International Version (1984 Edition). Holy Bible, New International Version®, NIV® Copyright © 1973, 1978, 1984 by Biblica, Inc.® Used by permission. All rights reserved worldwide.

Scripture marked NLT, was taken from the Holy Bible, New Living Translation, copyright © 1996, 2004, 2015 by Tyndale House Foundation. Used by permission of Tyndale House Publishers, Inc., Carol Stream, Illinois 60188. All rights reserved.

ISBN: 978-1-953241-51-1

Dedication

I dedicate this book to every person running, stressing, and trying to do it all in their own strength: *STOP! There is a better way, PAUSE with GOD and find it!*

I want to thank my family for always cheering me on. Oh, how I love you!

My husband, Joe; our two daughters, Briley Jo, and Gabriella; and my very first cheerleader, my mom.

To my extended family and friends (you know who you are). I'm so glad we do life together!

Thank you, Liberty and Willie Taylor, for your gift! And to Diana Robinson and Transformed Publishing for your talent and wisdom.

Ok. grab a pen!

Go to a quiet place!

And let's get started!

Acknowledgement

I would like to acknowledge
the goodness of GOD!
To GOD be all the
Glory, Honor, and Praise!
I want to acknowledge Holy Spirit
as He gave me this book
-YOU, HOLY SPIRIT
inspired this girl!

Table of Contents

Introduction

God has a real sense of humor. I suddenly awoke at 4:15 a.m. with the front cover of a book idea: *Life is Better in the Pause.* With a huge smile on my face, I pictured a lounge chair on a beautifully sunny day and the top of the Smoky Mountains. The bluest of skies flashed before me.

My attention peaked and a silent conversation started in my head that went something like this:

> *Life is better in the pause? A book? Funny, I don't do that. I don't 'pause' very well. God, but every time I have paused it has been absolutely 100% beneficial for me.*

I pondered for another few minutes. Then I decided I must get out of bed to grab a pen and paper. I knew if I didn't, the thoughts flowing through my mind would be gone the minute I fell back to sleep.

Done. I rose to my feet. I was up, out of bed, got my journal and pen, and I began to capture the message God was giving me.

Here we go! *It's like a treasure not yet found.* I had no idea what I'd find but, now I know God was prepared to serve the finest delicacy. I opened the treasure box lid and began searching, exploring, and discovering all God wanted me to know and share: *Life is Better in the Pause.*

1: What is a *Pause?*

My initial response to God was, *What? What is a pause?* I decided to take a *pause* from the conversation, grabbed my phone, and looked up the definition.

pause (noun) – 1: a temporary stop
2a: a break in a verse
  b: a brief suspension of the voice to indicate the limits and relations of sentences and their parts
3: temporary inaction especially as caused by uncertainty: HESITATION
4a: the sign denoting a fermata
  b: a mark (such as a period or comma) used in writing or printing to indicate or correspond to a pause of voice
5: a reason or cause for pausing (as to reconsider) *a thought that should give one pause*
6: a function of an electronic device that pauses a recording

pause (verb) – to stop temporarily: to linger for a time[1]

[1]"Pause." Merriam-Webster.com Dictionary, Merriam-Webster, https://www.merriam-webster.com/dictionary/pause. Accessed 11 Oct. 2023.

Life is Better in the *Pause*

The more I researched, the more synonyms I found, such as, stop, break, halt, standstill, respite, breathing space, hiatus, stay, lapse of time, delay, stop over, hold up, wait, hesitation, breather, lull, etc.

Wow! Look at all those definitions and synonyms, yippee! I love looking up definitions. It's like entering a new land for the very first time.

What a discovery! A pause is a temporary stop in action or speech. A pause is a stop, a break, a halt, a standstill. A pause is a lull, respite, breathing space. A pause is a hiatus, a stay, a lapse of time, a delay, a stopover, and a hold up. To pause is to wait, to hesitate. *Wow, even as I write I feel a slowing down of my pen.*

Words are powerful. Words have negative connotations or positive connotations. When I read the word, *hiatus*, I see it as good. When I read the word, *delay*, my immediate reaction is, *Oh no, I'll be late. I won't finish.*

What about you? What did you sense as you read this list? Which words pop out? And why? Let's linger for a time and think about these words used to describe what a *pause* is.

stop   standstill

break   respite

halt hold up

wait   hesitation

breather   lull

Pause

breathing space

delay   hiatus

stay   stop over

lapse of time

Your turn. Make your own list given the words describing a *pause*. Which words are positive for you? And which words have a negative connotation? Enjoy your discovery. Enjoy this *pause*.

Life is better in the pause.

Chapter 1: What?
Pause

Date

_____

_____

_____

_____

_____

_____

_____

_____

_____

_____

_____

_____

_____

Chapter 1: What?

Pause ———

Date

_____

_____

_____

_____

_____

_____

_____

_____

_____

_____

_____

_____

_____

_____

_____

_____

_____

_____

_____

_____

_____

_____

Chapter 1: What?
Pause

Date _____

_____

_____

_____

_____

_____

_____

_____

_____

_____

_____

_____

_____

_____

_____

_____

_____

_____

_____

_____

_____

2: Why is Life Better in the *Pause?*

I hope you enjoyed pondering in the *pause* of the previous chapter. In this next chapter, we will discover the *why. Why is life better in the pause?*

In this super-fast paced world, we all live in, I can think of immediate reasons why it is better to have a *pause*: a breather, a break, even a hiatus. As I share my personal reason, please intentionally think about yours. Journal space is available for you on pages 11-12.

My *pause* is for my spiritual, emotional, and physical well-being. When I'm in constant 'go' mode, after a while - *not* even a while, my brain becomes overloaded. Burnt out. Then a forced shutdown is generated.

Wouldn't we much rather *not* get to the point where our fuse is so overloaded that it blows? Or our body is so tired it cannot take one more agitation? What if we disciplined ourselves with purposeful *pauses* throughout our day? In other countries, siestas (rest in the afternoon) seem to work well for them. We will look at different ideas for *when* to pause, but for right now we're answering *why*.

Why? Because it is important for our well-being. It is good to *pause* to protect our mind, our will, and our emotions. Maybe *pausing* is a guarding of our heart. By design, our heart is a wellspring of life.

> Above all else, guard your heart, for it
> is the wellspring of life.
> -Proverbs 4:23 NIV

If we let worries consume us, our heart can easily become overwhelmed. The spring of our heart then begins to look and feel more like a stagnant pond. The word *if* expresses contingence on other factors. *If* we don't take necessary *pauses* to rest. *If* we don't take a breather, a stop. God wants us to *pause.* Each time I read the definition of *pause,* I further discover how vitally important the *pause* is in my life.

Have you been on 'go' overload? In what areas of your life would a *pause* be a great option for you right now? *Pause* and use this time to reflect. Pray, maybe even confess, whatever Holy Spirit reveals to you.

> Slow me down Lord to Your pace. Forgive my push, my busyness so I don't miss all the enjoyment You have for me in my life. Let me *pause* with you, God.

This is my prayer, friends. It can be your prayer, too.

Chapter 2: The Whys?

Pause ————

Date

_____

_____

_____

_____

_____

_____

_____

_____

_____

_____

_____

_____

_____

_____

_____

_____

_____

_____

_____

Chapter 2: The Whys?

Pause

Date _____

_____

_____

_____

_____

_____

_____

_____

_____

_____

_____

_____

_____

_____

_____

_____

_____

_____

_____

_____

_____

_____

3: When and How Long is a *Pause?*

Still right now, there is so much to consider when answering the question, *When do I pause?* Responses vary based on the synonym used. Think about the different reactions you have when asked:

> *When to stop?*
> *When to delay?*
> *When to rest?*

Every single noun used to define *pause* has its own answer. Let's take a few of these nouns and break them down.

STOP – BREAK - HALT

Q: *When* do I need to *stop*?
A: When I am burned out. When I am at the end of my rope.

Q: *When* does a *break* help?
A: When I'm not sure about a decision. I remember being in a meeting, options were presented, and I didn't know what to do. I asked for time. I took a *break*. I left the room, prayed, and got an answer. The break was necessary.

Q: *When* do we *halt*?

A: *Halt*, friends, that's a hard word for me. Based on my personal experiences, the word *halt* doesn't indicate a good situation. For me, it signifies, *I am in trouble - I need to stop - I need to get out.* There have been many times in my life when *halts* have happened that I had nothing to do with. I thank the powerful Holy Spirit for *halting* me and giving me clear direction, even change of direction when I needed it. For that I will always be grateful.

The inner voice of the Holy Spirit tells me things like, "It is not good here. Turn this way." Or, "This person is not trustworthy, leave." Being a Christian and walking with Jesus and having the powerful Holy Spirit on the inside enables me to feel secure because when I don't see something coming, He does. God, Jesus, and Holy Spirit see everything, and they protect me. They will protect you, too.

Here are some indicators we need to *halt*:
- ✓ Whenever we are fearful (relationships, career choices, moves, or any other fear).
- ✓ When we have lots of confusion.
- ✓ When we are feeling *forced* to move forward or to give an answer we don't *yet* have.

BREATHER – RESPITE - HIATUS

Q: *When* do I need a *breather?*
A: Maybe, throughout the day. Even just taking a short five-minute *breather* from what you are doing to step outside can make a world of difference.

Q: *When* do I take a *respite?*
A: A *respite* is a period of rest. As kids, we had recess at school. It was a fun break. I could not wait till recess! We adults need that, too. Find ways to take a *respite*. Break away from the routine of your day.

Q: *When* can I benefit from a *hiatus?*
A: A *hiatus* is taking a break for a little while. That 'little while' is between you and God. It might last a day, a week, or three weeks. It could be even longer.

I have been on *hiatus* throughout my life, some with no notice, because of injuries that could have been avoided if I had not pushed so hard. My sudden *hiatus* could have been stopped if I had listened to the promptings of the Holy Spirit. This is what you don't want. *Pause* before you have to. Take that vacation. It is good to take a *hiatus*, friends. Good for you and good for all the people around you.

Pause, linger here for a little while. What stirs in your spirit from this chapter? Use the space below to write down all that you need to.

Chapter 3:
When & How Long?

Pause

Date

_____
_____
_____
_____
_____
_____
_____
_____
_____
_____
_____
_____
_____
_____
_____

Chapter 3:
When & How Long?

Pause

Date _____

_____

_____

_____

_____

_____

_____

_____

_____

_____

_____

_____

_____

_____

_____

_____

_____

_____

_____

_____

_____

_____

_____

Chapter 3:
When & How Long?

Pause

Date _____

_____

_____

_____

_____

_____

_____

_____

_____

_____

_____

_____

_____

_____

_____

_____

_____

_____

_____

_____

_____

4: Using Your *Pause* Wisely

There is a *wise way* and there is a *foolish way*. If you are a Christian, the Book of Proverbs is a great book to read and meditate on regarding the wise and the foolish.

Often, we wait until we are forced into a *pause*. We hit our max. We are grumpy. We are exhausted. We are running on empty and finally *then* we see the need to stop.

Overwhelmingly, I have been *there* more often than I care to talk about. But honestly the truth is, I'm a doer. Resting is not my go-to. I enjoy being on the 'go'. I love hiking. I love climbing mountains, both in the natural as well as spiritually. I have consciously pushed myself past the limit just to see how much I can accomplish in one day.

Constantly striving and overworking is *not* God's desire for us. Knowing this truth ignited a desire in me for change. All change is a process, and my process has been ongoing for many years. I am learning. I have been foolish. And I have been forced out of commission as I've said in the previous chapter. Forced to stop. Forced to break. Then

I sulk. I have a bad attitude which produces nothing but bad results, friends.

It is always proven, once I get over my pity party, victory is just around the corner. There have been many times I needed to have a good heart to heart with God. I needed to repent for my stubborn rebellious ways. He is so good. God loves me through my foolishness. And He will love you through your foolishness. Thankfully, the older I get the wiser I become, and you can too.

Let's look at some wise ways to take a *pause* versus some unwise ways to *pause*. Below you'll see examples of wise and unwise *pauses*. I have noted some of my suggestions and then I have left space for you to fill in what comes to your mind.

Use this *pause*, wisely. Be honest. Be real. And learn.

Using a *Pause* Wisely:

1. Turn off social media and any other distractions.
2. Eat smart and explore types of fasts.
3. Get outdoors. Walk, hike, sit by a rushing creek. Choose something enjoyable and relaxing for you.

4. As I *pause,* I take my Bible, journal, and worship music because that is how I best hear from God.

List ways you could use a *pause* wisely:
1.

2.

3.

4.

Using a *Pause* Unwisely:

1. Scrolling the internet steals quiet time.
2. Eating lots of sugar loads me down.
3. Making calls, being busy, avoids quiet.
4. Watching meaningless movies or being a couch potato.

List ways you could use a *pause* unwisely:
1.

2.

3.

4.

Chapter 4:
Using Your *Pause* Wisely

Pause

Date ——————

———————————————————————————

———————————————————————————

———————————————————————————

———————————————————————————

———————————————————————————

———————————————————————————

———————————————————————————

———————————————————————————

———————————————————————————

———————————————————————————

———————————————————————————

———————————————————————————

———————————————————————————

———————————————————————————

———————————————————————————

———————————————————————————

———————————————————————————

———————————————————————————

———————————————————————————

———————————————————————————

———————————————————————————

———————————————————————————

Chapter 4:
Using Your *Pause* Wisely
Pause ———————

Date

_____

_____

_____

_____

_____

_____

_____

_____

_____

_____

_____

_____

_____

_____

_____

_____

_____

_____

_____

_____

_____

_____

_____

_____

Chapter 4:
Using Your *Pause* Wisely

Pause ——————

Date

_____

_____

_____

_____

_____

_____

_____

_____

_____

_____

_____

_____

_____

_____

_____

_____

_____

_____

_____

_____

_____

_____

_____

5: The BENEFITS of the Perfect *Pause*

There are benefits of a break, a rest, a halt, a delay, a breather, an intermission, a hiatus, a gap, a time-out, even from the two that may have a more negative connotation, a standstill or discontinuation.

When I am at a standstill, I have to seek God to know which way to go. In critical times, and even going through our daily routine, decisions must be made. Wisdom says seek the Lord's way and not our own way.

Do you see, friends? Do you see how we are pulling all the previous chapters together?

Let's look at discontinuation, as it relates to the perfect *pause*. Discontinuation is discontinuing something that needs to end. Something that most likely needed to end long ago. The *positive* is that an end gives room and opportunity for the *new* to come. It's eminent. *New* is on the way. Friends, yay for the discontinuation! Yay, for ending exhausting relationships. Yay, for the discontinuation of the job making you sick and abusing you.

The benefits of every break I have ever had were refreshment, rejuvenation, a reset, and a beginning again. In the small *pauses* my peace returned, anger didn't get the best of me or the situation at hand. In the small *pauses*, my joy was regained from the places it was stolen. Even a 5-minute breather is a go-to trusted game changer for me. When stress tries to get the best of me, I stop, I breathe, and I maintain my peace.

So, stop, breathe, intentionally take a *pause*; it is for your good. It is good to *pause*. As for us Christians, it is Biblical. Jesus often went alone to pray. Jesus withdrew to be refreshed. And if withdrawing, *pausing*, is good for Jesus then it is good for us.

There is a lot to digest from this final chapter, friends.

Pause...

Linger, alone with God.

Maybe you don't have the relationship with God, Jesus, and Holy Spirit that I have talked about. No problem, friends. There was a time having a relationship with God, Jesus, and Holy Spirit was foreign to me, too.

You have committed to reading this book if you have gotten this far. You and I have been engaged in a conversation, though we have never met face-to-face. Starting a relationship with God, Jesus, and Holy Spirit is a conversation away.

Here is *my* example but it does not have to be yours. You may use it as a model or have your own conversation in your time of prayer.

> God, I don't know You, but I would like to. I believe You created me. I want to understand who YOU are, who JESUS is and who Holy Spirit is. Please SHOW ME!

If this is your prayer, God heard you and HE WILL SHOW YOU.

Please email me at:
traceycruzauthor@gmail.com

I am willing to help you as you begin your new relationship. Our ministry is filled with resources.

As we conclude our journey together through, *Life is Better in the Pause,* I must say first of all, "Thank you, Lord for the wakeup call to bring this book to the table."

I want to encourage you, friends, I'm right alongside you, doing all that I can do to take the *pauses* I need to stay healthy - spiritually, physically, and emotionally because LIFE is truly BETTER in the *PAUSE*.

What would your benefits of *pausing* look like? Use the pages below to write.

Chapter 5:Your Benefits
Pause ———————
Date

_____

_____

_____

_____

_____

_____

_____

_____

_____

_____

_____

Chapter 5:Your Benefits
Pause ————

Date

_____

_____

_____

_____

_____

_____

_____

_____

_____

_____

_____

_____

_____

_____

_____

_____

_____

_____

_____

_____

_____

_____

_____

_____

Chapter 5:Your Benefits
Pause ———

Date

_____
_____
_____
_____
_____
_____
_____
_____
_____
_____
_____
_____
_____
_____
_____
_____
_____
_____
_____
_____

Conclusion

A STANDSTILL

As I complete this project, I am at a complete standstill, one of the synonyms of *pause*. Yet, my *standstill* is full of hope.

One of my favorite stories in the Bible is Moses leading the Israelites across the Red Sea. I find hope in my standstill.

> But Moses told the people, "Don't be afraid. Just stand still and watch the Lord rescue you today. The Egyptians you see today will never be seen again. The Lord himself will fight for you. Just stay calm."
>
> -Exodus 14:13-14 NLT

It does not say 'stand still', only. It says, "Just stand still and watch". *Stand still* and watch the deliverance of your God. We must follow the commanded action, *stand still,* to enter the standstill to witness the power of God, absent of our self-limitations. God is a promise keeper and it's for His name's sake.

We must remind ourselves: "God is going to show me what I need to do. He will deliver what I need."

Oh, those verses bring me such peace. God's promises bring me incredible hope! Knowing that my God will work my *not* knowing what to do assures me all will be well. Believing His promises gives me the sustaining power I need to endure until I watch God do what He has promised.

If you are at a standstill in your circumstances, be encouraged, there is a Deliverer, Almighty God. He sees, knows, and acts on behalf of His children.

The Israelites were up against the power of the Egyptian army. They were fearful, but God had already made a way! They saw and experienced it when they entered their standstill. God will continue to make a way for us too. So, stand still in your *pause* and watch God deliver. I know I am friends, and maybe, just maybe that will be my next book!

Until next time,

Hold on

Take as many Pauses as you need to

Be strong in the Lord

& Keep your joy!

About the Author

Tracey Cruz is a child-like and care-free kind of gal! Her daughters say, "Mom, you're always dancing with tulips in a field of flowers." Her husband is always reminding her, "Look both ways before crossing."

Tracey lovingly embraces their comments, and they cheer her on! Tracey is so thankful for the joy that remains in her spirit through ups & downs and highs & lows.

Tracey and her husband Joe have been in full-time ministry for over twenty-five years. They have raised two daughters and now reside in western North Carolina.

"Life is one big story. with many chapters and as the Lord says share. so shall I share."

-Tracey Cruz

Pause

Date

Pause

Date

_____

_____

_____

_____

_____

_____

_____

_____

_____

_____

_____

_____

_____

_____

_____

_____

_____

_____

_____

_____

_____

_____

_____

_____

_____

Pause

Date

Pause

Date

Pause ———

Date

Pause

Date

Pause

Date

Pause

Date

Life is Better in the *Pause*

Pause ———

Date

Pause

Date

Pause

Date

Pause

Date

Pause

Date

Pause

Date

Pause

Date

_____

_____

_____

_____

_____

_____

_____

_____

_____

_____

_____

_____

_____

_____

_____

_____

_____

_____

_____

_____

_____

_____

Pause

Date

Pause

Date

Pause

Date

Pause

Date _____

_____

_____

_____

_____

_____

_____

_____

_____

_____

_____

_____

_____

_____

_____

_____

_____

_____

_____

_____

_____

_____

_____

Pause

Date

_____

Pause

Date